Contents

Your Guide to the River

USING THEMED TEXT As you make your journey down the Yangtze you will find topic headings about that area of the river. These symbols show what the text is about.

🐇	**NATURE**	Plants, wildlife and the environment
📖	**HISTORY**	Events and people in the past
✋	**PEOPLE**	The lives and culture of local people
➡	**CHANGE**	Things that have altered the area
$	**ECONOMY**	Jobs and industry in the area

USING MAP REFERENCES Each chapter has a map that shows the section of the river we are visiting. The numbered boxes show exactly where a place of interest is located.

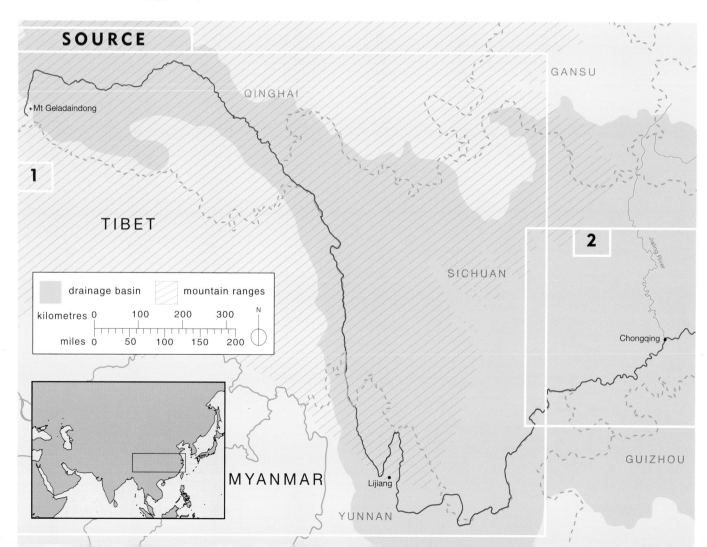

A RIVER JOURNEY

The Yangtze

Rob Bowden

HODDER
Wayland

an imprint of Hodder Children's Books

A RIVER JOURNEY

The Amazon	The Ganges
The Mississippi	The Nile
The Rhine	The Yangtze

For more information on this series and other Hodder Wayland titles, go to
www.hodderwayland.co.uk

A River Journey: The Yangtze

Commissioning Editor: Victoria Brooker
Book Editor: Deborah Fox
Book consultant: Tony Binns
Series consultant: Rob Bowden, EASI-Educational Resourcing

Cover design: Hodder Wayland   Book Design: Jane Hawkins
Picture Research: Shelley Noronha, Glass Onion Pictures
Maps: Tony Fleetwood

Series concept by: Environment and Society International –
Educational Resourcing

British Library Cataloguing in Publication Data
Bowden, Rob
  Yangtze. - (A river journey)
  1. Yangtze River (China) - Juvenile literature
  2. Yangtze River (China) - Geography - Juvenile literature
  I. Title
  915.1'2
ISBN 0750240393

Printed in China

Hodder Children's Books
A division of Hodder Headline Limited
338 Euston Road, London NW1 3BH

The website addresses (URLs) included in this book were valid at the time of going to press. However, because of the nature of the Internet, it is possible that some addresses may have changed, or sites may have changed or closed down since publication. While the author and Publisher regret any inconvenience this may cause readers, no responsibility for any such changes can be accepted by either the author or the Publisher.

The maps in this book use a conical projection, and so the indicator for North on the main map is only approximate.

Picture Acknowledgements

Cover: James Davis Travel Photography; title page Malcolm Watson/ Still Pictures; contents Chris Catton/ Oxford Scientific Films; 5 & 13 (bottom) James Davis Travel Photography; 6 Ian Cumming/Tibet Images; 7 Josef Müller, www.Open-Eye-Photography.de; 8 Philip Reeve/ Eye Ubiquitous; 9 (top) Julia Waterlow/ Eye Ubiquitous; 9 (bottom) Nick Bonetti/ Eye Ubiquitous; 10 Rhodri Jones/ Panos Pictures; 11 Julio Etchart/ Still Pictures; 12 (top) Michael S. Yamashita/Corbis (bottom) Popperfoto; 13 Martyn Evans/ Travel Ink; 14 Mark Henley/ Panos Pictures; 15 Mark Henley/ Panos PicturesPage 16 Nathan Smith/ Sylvia Cordaiy Photo Library; 17 David Lansdown/ Sylvia Cordaiy Photo Library; 18 Mark Henley/ Panos Pictures; 19 Camera Press; 20 Tony Binns/ Easi-er; 21 (top) Malcolm Watson/ Still Pictures (bottom) James Davis Worldwide Photographic Travel Library; 22/23 Mark Henley/ Panos Pictures; 24 (main) Guy Marks/ Axiom (inset) Liu Liqun/Corbis; 25 Liu Liqun/Corbis; 26 Bobby Yip/ Reuters/ Popperfoto; 27 (right) Jiri Rezac/ Axiom (bottom) Johnathan Smith/ Sylvia Cordaiy Photo Library; 28 & 29 Johnathan Smith/ Sylvia Cordaiy Photo; 30 Benoit Gysembergh/ Camera Press; 31 (top) Zhang dunhua-Imagine China (inset right) Bobby Yip/ Reuters/ Popperfoto; 32 Edward Parker; 33 (top) Stephen Coyne/ Sylvia Cordaiy Photo Library; 33 (inset) Julio Etchart/ Still Pictures (bottom) Alain le Garsmeur/ Panos Pictures; 34 N. Durrell McKenne/ Hutchinson Library; 35 Chris Catton/ Oxford Scientific Films; 36 Roland Seitre/ Still Pictures; 37 Tony Binns/Easi-er; 38 Richard Sharpley/ Hodder Wayland Picture Library; 39 (left) Tiziana and Gianni Baldizzone/Corbis (right) Gordon Clements/ Hodder Wayland Picture Library; 40 Robert Francis/ Hutchinson Library; 41 (left) Ric Ergenbright/Corbis (bottom) James Davis Worldwide Photographic Travel Library; 42 Catherine Platt/ Panos Pictures; 43 Earth Satellite Corporation/ Science Photo Library; 44/45 Mark Henley/ Impact

The Journey Ahead

The Yangtze is Asia's longest river, so long in fact that its Chinese name 'Chang Jiang' means 'Long River'. The Yangtze begins its 6,300 kilometre journey high in the Qinghai-Tibet plateau of western China. After crossing the plateau, the young river crashes over rapids and takes wild turns as it cascades 1,600 kilometres through steep mountain valleys. At Yibin the Yangtze leaves the mountains. Several major tributaries join it, including the Min and Jialing rivers, as the Yangtze passes through the Sichuan Basin.

From Chongqing the river valley is wide enough to support several major settlements. However, it then narrows again at the dramatic Three Gorges, soon to be flooded by an enormous dam. From Yichang the Yangtze opens out into vast plains that stretch all the way to Nanjing. The delta beyond Nanjing is heavily urbanized, especially around Shanghai, just before the Yangtze ends its journey in the East China Sea.

Let's begin our river journey with a flight over the remote upper reaches of the Yangtze. We land at Lijiang and from there head by road into one of the world's deepest gorges!

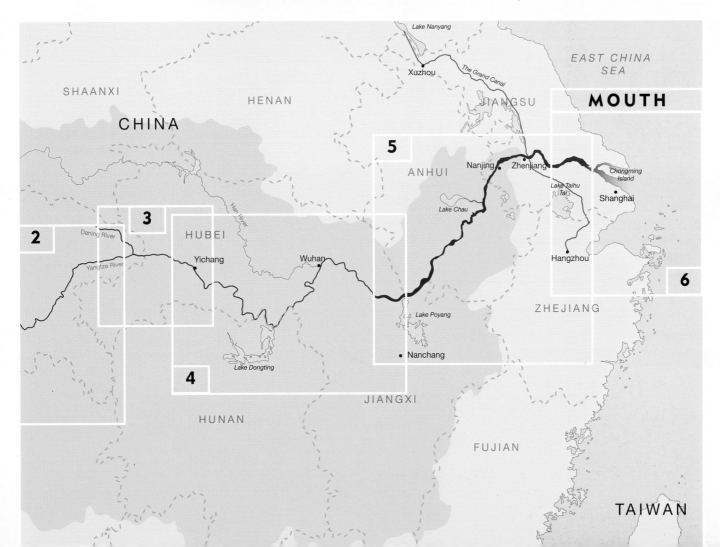

Map labels:
- Mt Geladaindong
- QINGHAI
- TIBET
- Yangtze River
- SICHUAN
- INDIA
- MYANMAR
- Lijiang
- YUNNAN
- km 0 100 200
- miles 0 50 100 150

1. Mountains and Gorges

FLYING OVER THE QINGHAI-TIBET plateau you can see how vast and isolated this region is. Our flight path follows the Yangtze for about 1,400 kilometres as it falls from its source into deep mountain valleys, almost disappearing from view at times. We land at Lijiang and take a bus trip along the steep roads to the spectacular Tiger Leaping Gorge. We learn a little about how people survive in this difficult environment and return to Lijiang to experience the unique local culture, before moving on.

Below: Herders living on the vast Tibetan plateau mainly keep yaks. Their thick coats help withstand the bitter cold of winter.

Right: Firewood is the main source of fuel for local people, but collecting it has had dramatic impacts on the environment.

📖 HISTORY *Mysterious source*

Finding the source of a river like the Yangtze is not an easy task. There are so many streams and rivers joining it that each one is a potential source! For many years people believed the source to be the Min Jiang (Jiang means 'river' in Chinese). Then, in the mid-seventeenth century, a Chinese geographer discovered that another river, the Jinsha Jiang, was even longer. Jinsha Jiang became the new name for the upper section of the Yangtze.

The true source of the Yangtze was still a mystery however. Then, in 1976, a small glacier-fed lake called Qemo Lake at the foot of Mount Geladaindong, which is 6,559 metres high, was discovered. The lake was named as the source.

🐇 NATURE *Fragile lands*

The rainy season in the upper Yangtze is between April and August, and heavy storms are common during this period. Rainwater pours down mountain slopes and floods the plateau as it rushes to find the shortest route to the river. Because of the fragile land in this region, the surging rainwater erodes large amounts of soil. Human actions have made this problem even worse. Local people remove trees to use as fuel or for building, and livestock grazing removes the vegetation, leaving soils unprotected when it rains heavily.

In September 2001 the government announced a set of actions to reduce erosion in the upper Yangtze. The measures included educating people about soil conservation and improving local laws to protect the land from misuse. The government will also monitor environmental protection in the upper Yangtze more often.

💲 ECONOMY *New opportunities*

After flying over the Yangtze headwaters, we land at the new airport in Lijiang. The airport opened in 1994. It has brought new opportunities and economic growth to this region.

Tourism has become big business around Lijiang, an ancient city famous for its narrow streets and traditional mountain culture. For us, like many visitors, Lijiang is also the starting point for a visit to Tiger Leaping Gorge MAP REF: 1 . We take a bus to the gorge via the small town of Shigu located on the first major bend of the Yangtze. From Shigu the drive into the gorge is a thrilling adventure along a narrow road cut into the mountainside. There is only a small wall

Above: Few people live in the isolated mountain gorges of the upper Yangtze. We can see their villages from our plane.

between our bus and the 200-metre drop to the valley below! The road was completed in 1997 as part of a plan to encourage tourism in Yunnan province.

As we make our final descent into Tiger Leaping Gorge, you can see that local people have taken advantage of the growth in tourism too. The 1,000 steps between the viewpoint and the river's edge are lined with refreshment and souvenir stalls. There is even a service to carry you up the steps in a sedan chair if you get a little tired, but spare a thought for those carrying you!

NATURE *Leap of faith*

I think you'll agree that Tiger Leaping Gorge is one of the world's most spectacular natural sights. For seventeen kilometres the Yangtze is squeezed between towering natural walls and it falls about 300 metres over eighteen sets of furious rapids. If you look up, you can see the gorge walls reaching, almost vertically, for the sky above. In places they are over 3,000 metres high, making this one of the world's deepest gorges.

The gorge has been cut from the surrounding land by the force of the falling river water and the rocks and debris it carries. The rapids are formed where harder bands of rock cross the river bed and resist the force of the river. One of these harder rocks, Tiger Leaping Stone, sits above the water at a point where the gorge is just thirty metres wide. The stone and the gorge are named after a legend that tells of a tiger leaping across the gorge whilst being chased by hunters – a true leap of faith!

Right: The beauty of Tiger Leaping Gorge attracts many visitors. Below: The Yangtze crashes past tourists at Tiger Leaping Stone with incredible force!

Mountain farming

As we leave Tiger Leaping Gorge we can see that a lot of the land in this area is farmed. Because there is so little flat land here, local farmers create their own by digging narrow terraces along the hillsides. This gives the local landscape its distinctive stepped appearance. Farmers remove stones from the plot and place them around its edges, which reduces soil erosion during heavy rain. If they need extra water, they connect small channels to the mountain streams that criss-cross this area. Most of this work is done by hand, but on the larger plots farmers sometimes use water buffalo to plough the land before they plant it.

Farmers in this area grow a mixture of crops. They grow some, like maize, potatoes and rice, for themselves. This is known as 'subsistence farming'. They grow other crops to sell; they are known as 'cash crops'. Cash crops in this region include sunflowers and rapeseed – grown for their oil – and tobacco.

Below: Farmers have become experts at building terraces into mountainsides in order to grow crops. This technique also reduces soil erosion.

NATURE *Trees of life*

One of the problems with mountain farming is that people remove trees to create fields or use the trees as fuel or for building. Trees are important because the canopy (the branches and leaves) protects the soil from the driving rain and the tree roots hold the soil together. When trees are removed, rain simply washes down the mountainsides, taking much of the soil with it. The soil is deposited in the Yangtze, adding to the natural sediment already carried by the river. The channel becomes shallower, which means that the river holds less water. There is then a much greater risk of flooding.

In 1998 the Yangtze experienced terrible flooding, the worst for forty-four years. Deforestation was blamed because

Above: Once the trees have been removed, steep slopes can quickly be eroded.

it had caused soil erosion in the upper reaches of the river. Since the 1950s, forests along the Yangtze have halved in size. Environmentalists have been complaining for a long time that the clearance of trees would cause greater flooding of the Yangtze.

Finally, following the floods of 1998, the government acted. Strict new laws have now been introduced to reduce tree clearance and local people are being educated about the importance of trees for flood control. Tree-planting schemes have also been introduced to reduce erosion and rainwater run-off in some of the worst affected areas.

Above: The Naxi orchestra has been in existence for hundreds of years. Left: A Dongba (holy man) writing in the Naxi's unique pictorial script. The Naxi are the last people in the world to still use pictorial scripts.

PEOPLE The Naxi of Lijiang

Few people live in the isolated mountainous environment of the upper Yangtze. One group of people that we will meet however is the Naxi. Originally from Tibet, the Naxi have lived in the area around Lijiang for over 1,000 years. Today there are about 250,000 Naxi people. They grow crops like rice and wheat and they also breed horses that are regarded as some of the strongest in China. In recent years the Naxi have become involved in tourism as visitors from China and abroad come to learn more about their unique culture.

The Naxi religion is known as 'Dongba', named after the shaman, or holy men, who teach and preserve its traditions. Dongba religion is centred on the belief that all natural things have a soul. The Naxi worship the sun and moon, the clouds and mountains, and, of course, the Yangtze itself. Today, the

Above: Lijiang is being rebuilt following a major earthquake in 1996. Money from increased tourism in China is helping to fund the rebuilding.

→ CHANGE *Rebuilding Lijiang*

On 3 February 1996, the Lijiang area suffered a major earthquake. Over 250 people were killed and more than 4,000 were seriously injured. In Lijiang itself, about a third of the town was destroyed, including some of its oldest buildings. As the area is rebuilt, the Chinese government is encouraging its development as a major tourist centre. They believe that the combination of the spectacular Yangtze gorges and the fascinating Naxi culture will make Lijiang a key centre for China's rapidly growing tourist industry.

They may be right, but others are concerned that developing the area for tourism may spoil its charms and turn the Naxi people into little more than a living exhibition.

Dongba spend many hours translating ancient scripts that experts believe date back to the tenth century. Their writing is actually a series of pictures instead of letters.

Music is also a big part of Naxi culture and a visit to Lijiang is not complete without enjoying a performance by the famous Naxi orchestra. The orchestra is said to have started in the thirteenth century when a great emperor called Kublai Khan donated instruments to the Naxi after they had helped his army to cross the Yangtze. Most of the instruments are either strummed or hammered and produce beautiful, haunting sounds.

We take off from Lijiang and follow the Yangtze out of the mountains and across the Sichuan Basin beyond Yibin. We land in Chongqing where we can finally take to the river!

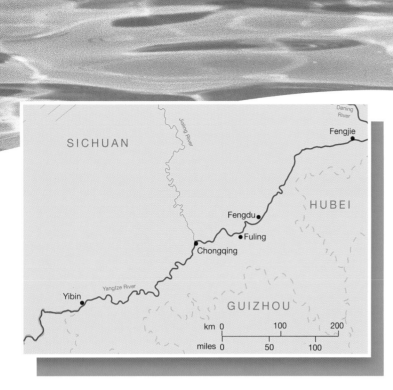

2. The Sichuan Basin

AS WE LAND IN CHONGQING we have already followed the Yangtze for about two-thirds of its journey. It is at Chongqing, however, that the river really comes to life. We spend some time exploring this bustling city and we sample some of the local food. The port is the centre of Chongqing's economy and we discover the importance of the Yangtze for trade in this part of China. As we continue our journey towards Fengjie, we pass through an area that will soon be flooded by a major dam being built downstream. We consider the changes this will mean for people living here and the problems it may cause.

Below: The view from one of the cable cars that carry people between the mainland and the peninsula shows just how fast Chongqing is growing.

Above: The steep and crowded path to Chaotianmen Docks. Balancing cargo on these poles is a real skill that takes years to master.

 NATURE *Waters meet*

Chongqing marks a major change in the Yangtze. The river is slower and has widened since leaving the narrow mountain gorges. Several tributaries join the Yangtze as it approaches the city. In Chongqing itself, the Yangtze is joined by the Jialing river, which began life about 720 kilometres to the north. The hilly peninsula of land between the confluence of the two rivers is the commercial centre of Chongqing. As the population has grown, however, the city has spread beyond the peninsula on to the land beyond both the Yangtze and Jialing rivers. One of the most interesting ways to travel between the peninsula and the mainland is by cable car. There are two cable cars, one across each river, and they both give fantastic views of this thriving river city.

 PEOPLE *Crowded streets*

Chongqing has been the most important city in south-western China for many years. Its continued importance to modern China was made clear in 1997 when it was separated from Sichuan province and made into its own municipality. Chongqing is also the most populated city in south-western China – it was home to nearly six million people in 2002. A further twenty-four million live in the municipal area, many of them in the towns and villages that line the Yangtze and Jialing rivers.

With so many people, the streets of Chongqing are extremely crowded, especially around the docks. Because the streets are so steep, there are no bicycles – the normal way to transport goods in Chinese cities. It's an unusual sight for us to see people carrying things in baskets slung from poles balanced across their shoulders. It takes some skill to negotiate the narrow streets!

Above: Chongqing has become a centre for vehicle production in China. The Yangtze is a vital route for transporting finished goods to the rest of China.

$ ECONOMY   *Industrial heartland*

Chongqing is an area rich in natural resources. It has China's biggest reserves of natural gas. It also has large quantities of coal, rock salt and precious metals, including mercury and manganese. This reason, together with the city's position on the banks of the Yangtze, makes Chongqing an ideal location for an industrial city. From here raw materials and finished goods can be transported to Shanghai and the East China Sea.

The centre of activity in Chongqing is Chaotianmen Docks. From here, millions of tonnes of cargo are moved up and down the river, or sent to the railways and roads that link Chongqing to other parts of western China.

Many of Chongqing's main industries are based on its natural resources, but, since the mid 1980s, manufacturing has also become important. Vehicle production has been particularly successful. By the late 1990s Chongqing's factories were producing over 124,000 cars and other vehicles and 1,785,000 motorcycles a year! The success of Chongqing's industries is evident from the rapid growth of the city. Look at the huge cranes dotting the landscape! Each new building seems bigger than the last, reaching ever higher into the sky. There is a downside to this success however. Emissions from factories and traffic cause high levels of air pollution. Chongqing is often covered in a permanent choking haze. Pollution from Chongqing also affects the Yangtze as we'll soon find out.

✋ PEOPLE *Sichuan food*

Before leaving Chongqing, we must sample the local Sichuan cooking. One of the main ingredients in Sichuan cooking is chilli pepper and many of the most popular dishes are hot and spicy. Chicken, duck, fish, pork, vegetables and rice, of course, are all found on the menu. There are also more unusual items such as braised frog and snake! The speciality though is Sichuan hotpot, known locally as 'huoguo'. Diners cook meat and vegetables at their table in a bubbling pot of spiced chicken stock. Once cooked, the food is flavoured with spicy oil, salt and chilli powder. Hotpot originated in Chongqing and is found in most of the open-air cafés where people gather to socialize and share a meal. Sitting in one of Chongqings cafés is a great way to watch life go by and meet local people.

Below: Sichuan hotpot is a local speciality. Cooking and eating it together is a great social occasion.

Rising waters

A funicular railway takes us down to the muddy riverbanks and the passenger ferry that will carry us downstream to Fengjie. As the ferry sets off, the strong current swiftly carries us away. Looking back you can see how Chongqing is preparing itself for the effects of rising waters in this part of the Yangtze. New roads are being built high above the current river level and new buildings are now growing upwards instead of outwards across land that will soon be flooded. High on the riverbanks new flood defences give some idea of how much water levels could rise. But why are the waters rising?

The reason is that by 2009 this area will become part of the world's biggest reservoir. The reservoir will stretch 632 kilometres downstream from Chongqing to the enormous Three Gorges Dam being built at Sandouping. We visit the dam later in our journey, but it is in this area of the Yangtze that many of dam's effects will be felt. Water levels are expected to rise by up to one hundred metres behind the dam wall. They will permanently flood any land below this new water line. The Yangtze between

Left: Shibaozhai pagoda is known as the 'Pearl of the Three Gorges'. When the Three Gorges Dam is complete, the water will totally submerge these houses below it.

Chongqing and Sandouping will be changed forever and much of what we see on this stretch of the journey may be under water in a few years' time!

$ PEOPLE *Moving up!*

The rising waters of the Three Gorges reservoir will not only flood land, they will also flood over 1,300 villages, 326 towns and 19 cities along this stretch of the Yangtze. To protect these communities from the rising waters, China is now moving up to 1.9 million people to new settlements above the water line. This is one of the biggest resettlement programmes the world has ever seen. Resettlement began in 1997 and will continue until the dam is finished in 2009. In some parts of the river, settlements are moving to higher ground, as we saw in Chongqing, but in other areas whole towns and villages have been completely relocated.

Despite financial help from the government, many people are unhappy about being moved from their homes. Many have lived in them all their lives. The Chinese believe in worshipping their ancestors. To watch their ancestral homes disappear under water is especially hard.

Right: Villagers have to relocate because their villages will soon be under water. Not all people are happy to move however.

The 'Golden Waterway'

Seventy per cent of water transport in China is on the Yangtze and eighty per cent of all the cargo transported by river, is on the Yangtze. Its importance to the Chinese economy has earned it the name of the 'Golden Waterway'. However, between Chongqing and Yichang, which is downstream of the new reservoir, the Yangtze's waters are too shallow for larger trade vessels to navigate. This is because the river bed has numerous areas of sand or gravel that build up and reduce the depth of the river. These areas are known as shoals.

Soon the shoals will be a problem of the past though. The new reservoir behind the Three Gorges Dam will increase the water depth dramatically. Large ocean-going vessels, ten times the size of current ones, will be able to navigate the complete waterway between Chongqing and the East China Sea. The improvements in navigation are expected to increase river traffic on the 'Golden Waterway' by up to five times and reduce the cost of shipping by about a third. This will bring new trade and wealth to the people living alongside the Yangtze and especially around major ports such as Chongqing.

NATURE *A dirty business*

Although the Yangtze is vital to the Chinese economy, many of the activities that take place along its banks are extremely dirty. The heavy industries you can see, such as

Below: When the Three Gorges Dam is complete, vessels up to ten times the size of these will be able to safely travel along the Yangtze.

steel and chemical factories, produce large quantities of waste. Agriculture is not much better. Fertilizers and pesticides used on the fields spread into the wider environment. A lot of this pollution finds its way into the Yangtze, which has major impacts on the river.

In January 2002 one study estimated that over six million tonnes of rubbish and almost ten million tonnes of industrial solid waste were dumped into the upper Yangtze every year. If liquid waste from homes, sewers and industries is included,

Above: The huge amount of domestic waste produced along the Yangtze has a disastrous effect on the quality of the river water. Industry generates even more pollution.

then the figures are even higher. Chongqing alone spews over a billion tonnes of waste water into the Yangtze every year, ninety per cent of it from industrial sources. The government has been trying to clean up the Yangtze by spending US$4.8 billion on waste controls from 2002 to 2012. Though this is welcomed, some fear it may be too little too late!

Our ferry calls at the port town of Fuling and passes Fengdu, before arriving in Fengjie. We transfer to a tourist cruise boat for our journey to the Three Gorges.

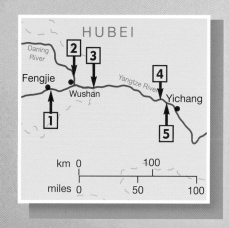

3. The Three Gorges

FENGJIE IS A BUSY LITTLE TOWN at one end of the Yangtze's famous Three Gorges. We join other tourists on board one of the many cruise boats heading downstream to Yichang. The water here is already beginning to rise, but the Three Gorges are still a breathtaking sight. At the end of the first gorge in Wushan, we take a short diversion along the Daning River to explore the beautiful Lesser Three Gorges. Back on the Yangtze we reach the site of the new dam at Sandouping as we leave the last of the Three Gorges. We can't stop at the dam as it is a restricted area, so we continue towards Yichang, passing through the smaller Gezhou Dam on the way.

Right: The stunning beauty and dramatic scale of the entrance to Qutang Gorge has enchanted travellers for centuries.

NATURE *The Three Gorges*

The Three Gorges were formed by a vast inland sea that carved its way through a series of faults in the earth's surface. This all took place around seventy million years ago, but the dramatic results are all around us as we zig-zag our way through the limestone gorges for the next 129 kilometres. Sections of the gorge stretch almost vertically above us, rising as jagged peaks up to 1,200 metres high. In places the rocks have formed into strange shapes, many of which have been given interesting names. In Xiling Gorge, for example, you will find rocks called 'Ox Liver', 'Horse Lung' and 'Sword'. The steepest slopes have no vegetation on them, but the lower slopes are covered in forests or grassland.

As the Yangtze passes through the Three Gorges it collects water and sediment from several small tributaries.

In places the tributaries have cut deep ravines in the walls of the gorge that in millions of years could become gorges in their own right. Many of the smaller tributaries will be flooded as this part of the river rises behind the Three Gorges Dam downstream. You can see the level the water is expected to reach indicated by white markers high on the valley sides. Other markers indicate the height of previous floods – one of the main reasons the dam is being built is to prevent flooding as we will soon discover.

💲 ECONOMY *Gorge cruises*

Most visitors see the Three Gorges as we are, by taking a cruise along the Yangtze. Some of the boats are extremely luxurious and travel non-stop between Chongqing and Wuhan, downstream of the Three Gorges. As travel to China becomes easier, it is expected to become the world's number one tourist destination by 2020. The Three Gorges will be one of its top attractions and several tour companies have already ordered new boats to meet the demand.

The first gorge heading downstream is the impressive Qutang Gorge MAP REF: 1. It may be the shortest gorge at just eight kilometres long, but its near vertical mountainsides provide a grand entrance to the gorges. High up on one side is an old towpath that was once used to tow boats through the gorge before navigation was improved. At the end of Qutang Gorge we moor at Wushan and take a short diversion along the Daning river to visit the Lesser Three Gorges MAP REF: 2. Though lesser by name, they are equally, if not more, spectacular and many visitors rate them as the highlight of a Yangtze cruise.

📖 HISTORY *Yangtze dragons*

Back on the Yangtze we continue into Wu Gorge MAP REF: 3, famous for its Yangtze river dragons! Legend has it that twelve wild dragons created chaos in the river and its gorge, leading to floods and destruction wherever they went. Yao Ji, a daughter of the Queen Mother of the West, defeated the dragons and then turned herself and her eleven sisters into twelve peaks (six on each side of the gorge) to safely guide boatmen and protect local villagers. Many other myths and legends are told about the Three

Gorges, but the story of Yao Ji is one of the best known. As we pass through Wu Gorge, you may spot Goddess Peak, said to be Yao Ji herself in the shape of a kneeling maiden.

📖 HISTORY *Safe passage*

The final gorge, Xiling MAP REF: 4, is also the longest at seventy-six kilometres. In the past it was also the most dangerous of the gorges and countless boatmen and travellers drowned in its turbulent and rocky waters. Then, in the 1950s, the government improved navigation by using dynamite to blast away the dangerous rocks creating a safe passage for boats. Today, we follow other river traffic in a convoy between markers showing the safest route.

Left: Tourists look ahead as they approach the entrance to Qutang gorge. Left inset: Many of The Three Gorges cruise boats are like floating hotels, carrying up to 260 passengers. The new ones are set to be even bigger! Right: Local legends on how Wu Gorge was formed focus on its dramatic rock formations.

➡ CHANGE *Another Great Wall!*

The Great Wall of China is undoubtedly China's most famous landmark, but it is soon to be joined by another Great Wall, this time across the Yangtze. As we leave Xiling Gorge, we see the 'wall' for the first time ... the Three Gorges Dam, being built at the town of Sandouping MAP REF: 5 . When it is finished in 2009, it will stretch two kilometres across the Yangtze and stand 185 metres high – as high as a tower of forty double-decker buses!

The dam has been a cause of great argument since it was started in 1994.

Supporters of the dam point out that it will control flooding on the Yangtze. During the twentieth century, floods killed over 320,000 people, 4,000 of them during the last serious floods in 1998. The dam will also generate hydro-electric power (HEP) for China's growing energy needs. It will provide the equivalent of eighteen nuclear power stations or the burning of forty million tonnes of coal a year. The people against the dam claim that building it will damage the environment and disrupt the lives of local people. They believe a series of smaller dams would have less impact. They are also worried about what might happen if the dam were ever damaged by a major flood or an earthquake like the one that struck Lijiang in 1996.

Below: The model and artist's impression help people to understand what the Three Gorges Dam will look like when it is finished in 2009.

Right: The Three Gorges Dam is one of the world's biggest-ever construction sites. Can you imagine trying to organize up to 30,000 workers!

Whatever you think of the dam and the changes it will bring, you can't fail to be impressed by its enormous size! It will be the biggest in the world when it is finished. As we pass the site you will see some of the 30,000 workers, 40 cranes and hundreds of trucks involved in this amazing project.

 NATURE *Sediment trap*

The Yangtze carries 500 to 700 million tonnes of sediment downstream every year – the fourth biggest load of all the world's rivers. Normally sediment is deposited along the length of the river or washed out to sea. Experts are concerned, however, that the new dam could become a giant sediment trap, reducing the depth of the river and causing greater flooding as far upstream as Chongqing. Shipping would also be affected and, in the worst case, the build-up of sediment and rising waters could turn the Three Gorges Dam into a giant waterfall!

Engineers have built a series of twenty-three sluice gates in the dam wall to flush the sediment downstream, but no-one is sure if they will work as they've never been used on a river with so much sediment.

Our journey downstream is blocked by another dam – the Gezhou Dam.
To pass below it, we enter a ship-lock.

4.The Yangtze Plains

AFTER NEGOTIATING THE ship-lock through the Gezhou Dam, our cruise boat leaves us in Yichang. We catch another passenger ferry to take us further downstream. The Yangtze is slowing now and becomes almost sluggish as it meanders through the low flat land of the Yangtze Plains. Flooding is a big threat in this region and people have to combat it. A short diversion takes us to Lake Dongting, China's second largest lake. In the industrial city of Wuhan we visit one of its textile factories.

Below: The landscape below the Gezhou Dam is much flatter and the river begins to slowly meander around enormous bends.

$ ECONOMY *Ship staircase*

The Gezhou Dam MAP REF: 1 is itself a giant
at 2.6 kilometres wide and 70 metres high! To
pass below it we enter one of three ship-
locks, two of which are among the biggest in
the world. They can lower or raise ships of up
to 10,000 tonnes! The locks are vital to
navigation on the Yangtze and to the growth
of the economy in this region. Similar ship-
locks are now being built at the Three Gorges
Dam upstream. When it is completed, this
section of the Yangtze will become one of the
most advanced shipping passages in the
world – a sort of giant ship staircase.

Going downstream, we enter the lock at
the level of the river above the dam. The
enormous doors close behind us and the
water in the lock chamber is slowly released.
After just over an hour we reach the level of
the river below the dam. The doors finally

Above: The ship-locks in the Gezhou Dam are
huge. Navigating them is a memorable event for
tourists enjoying a Yangtze river cruise.

open. We dock in Yichang, an important
transport centre on this part of the Yangtze.

NATURE *Plains and meanders*

As our ferry leaves Yichang, the landscape
changes dramatically. We are entering the
Yangtze floodplain, an enormous area of flat,
low-lying land. The floodplain has been built
up over hundreds of thousands of years as
the Yangtze has deposited sediment on to
the surrounding land during its annual
flooding. The build up of sediment slows the
river and it begins to wind its way across the
floodplain in a series of bends called
meanders. In places, old meanders are cut off
from the main channel and form isolated
patches of water known as ox-bow lakes.

$ ECONOMY *Living with risk*

The sediment of the floodplain is very rich in nutrients and makes extremely fertile farmland. You can see more farming here than at any point on our journey so far. But the millions of people living here also live with a real risk – the risk of flooding. If the Yangtze rises too high, then it naturally spills on to the surrounding floodplain as it has for thousands of years. With so many people now living and farming on this land, there is a constant battle between them and the Yangtze. There are many examples where the Yangtze seems to be winning this battle. In 1998, for example, the Yangtze flooded around 197,000 hectares of farmland (equivalent to about 280,000 football pitches).

But people in this area have been fighting back for hundreds of years. One example of their struggle is the 182-kilometre Jingjiang levee **MAP REF: 2**, which was started in AD 345 – over 1,650 years ago! The levee is a wall of earth along the bank of the river that protects eight million people, two major cities and 800,000 hectares of farmland. As we journey down the Yangtze you will see many more levees protecting the people of the floodplains. In fact there are now 3,600 kilometres of major levees and 30,000 kilometres of smaller ones along the Yangtze.

Below: The fertile floodplains provide rich farmland, but they can also ruin farmers when the land floods after a period of heavy rain.

Above: The army and volunteers struggle to mend a burst levee protecting Jingjiang in 1999.
Right: Boats were more useful than cars on the streets of Jiujiang following the devastating floods of 1998.

 PEOPLE *Drastic action*

Although levees are built to protect people and their land, in serious floods they can sometimes give way. If this happens suddenly, it can have dramatic consequences. A wall of water rushes across the low-lying land below. During the 1998 floods, levees in various sections of the river gave way and caused massive damage. The city of Jiujiang (downstream of Wuhan) was badly affected when a forty-metre gap opened up in the levee protecting it. The Yangtze poured in, flooding the homes of 40,000 people with almost two metres of water.

To avoid similar damage elsewhere, the government decided to take drastic action. It removed around 330,000 people from their homes in the upper Yangtze so that nearby levees could be broken and the land flooded. Although drastic, this action reduced the risk of flooding in the heavily populated and important industrial areas of the middle and lower Yangtze.

NATURE *The shrinking lake*

A few kilometres downstream of the Jingjiang levee we reach Lake Dongting. It is the second largest lake in China, covering about 2,740 square kilometres – almost twice the area of London! One hundred and fifty years ago, however, Lake Dongting was double that size! So what has happened?

Over the years, the Yangtze's floodwaters have been pushed downstream by the Jingjiang levee instead of flooding on to the surrounding plains. As the waters arrive at Lake Dongting, they slow and deposit the sediment they are carrying. Over the years the deposition has caused the lake to gradually silt up. Farmers in this region have made the problem worse. They have built small dykes around the edge of the lake to reclaim land as the water evaporates.

In 1999 the government announced that farmers should break down some of these dykes. This would help store water during serious floods as part of China's national flood prevention plan.

$ ECONOMY *Transport and textiles*

When we reach Wuhan the Yangtze is joined by its longest tributary, the Han river. The Han rises 1,540 kilometres to the north west (above Chongqing on our main map).

Wuhan itself is a major transport centre and provides links between the river, road and rail networks. You can see how lively the streets are with the bustle of people and goods transferring between different forms of transport. At one time the only way

Below: Land reclaimed for farming has contributed to a fall in Lake Dongting's water levels.

Above: This road and rail bridge across the Yangtze has increased Wuhan's importance as a transport centre.

Right: Thousands of people, especially women, are employed in Wuhan's textile industries.

to cross the Yangtze, which is 1,500 metres wide at this point, was by ferry. Even rail traffic was taken across by ferry until 1957 when the Changjiang Bridge was built across the Yangtze. A second bridge was completed in 1995. Today Wuhan provides the vital north-south rail link across the Yangtze, linking Beijing (the Chinese capital) in the north to Guangzhou and Hong Kong in the south.

The good transport links, and its location in one of China's main cotton-growing regions, make Wuhan a natural centre for the textile industry. Wuhan's factories export fabric and clothes all over the world. China is one of the world's biggest producers of textiles. Perhaps your clothes were made in China? In 2001 China exported textiles worth over US$53 billion, twenty per cent of all China's export earnings.

Wuhan is also an industrial city with iron and steel works, vehicle production and shipbuilding.

We leave Wuhan on one of the many grain barges heading downstream into one of China's most important farming regions.

ANHUI

1

Zhenjiang

Nanjing

Lake Chao

Yangtze River

Lake Taihu Tai

The Grand Canal

Yangtze River

Hangzhou

Lake Poyang

JIANGXI

ZHEJIANG

km 0   100   200

miles 0   50   100

5. Land of Fish and Rice

DOWNSTREAM OF WUHAN, WE enter the 'Land of Fish and Rice'. As the name suggests, farming and fishing are incredibly important here. In fact, the area between here and the Yangtze delta produces around seventy per cent of China's paddy rice, forty per cent of its grain, and over half of its freshwater fish catch.

We'll learn more about rice-farming and fishing and look at the impact fishing has had on wildlife in the Yangtze. Nanjing, the ancient capital of China, is our next stop. Then we leave our barge when the Yangtze meets the Grand Canal at Zhenjiang.

Below: This farmer is feeding fish kept in special ponds. Fish farming, or aquaculture, is an ancient, but fast-growing practice in China.

$ ECONOMY   *Farming for fish*

Fishing is an important activity along this stretch of the Yangtze and in the numerous lakes, such as Poyang and Chao, found nearby. In 1998 Chinese fishermen caught almost 2.3 million tonnes of freshwater fish, which was over a quarter (28.5 per cent) of the world total. This was by far the biggest catch of any country in the world and over half of it came from the Yangtze!

Various fishing methods are used on the river, but one of the more unusual is the use of tamed cormorants. Cormorants are expert fish-catching birds. They dive from the edge of fishing boats to catch the fish underwater. They are prevented from swallowing the fish by a ring placed around their necks.

China also leads the world in fish-farming, or aquaculture and, in 1998, produced over twenty-seven million tonnes. Although part of this production was

Above: Fishing with the help of cormorants is an unusual fishing technique that has survived through generations of change.

exported, much is eaten locally. In fact, the average Chinese person eats over seventeen kilograms of farmed fish every year! This compares with just 2.1 kilograms per person per year in the rest of the world. Don't worry, we'll have a chance to try the local fish dishes as we travel through this region.

You may have noticed that many farmers keep fish ponds on their land. This is partly to earn money, but the ponds have other uses too. They supply water for crops and their sediment provides a rich natural fertilizer for the fields. In turn, farm waste is added to the ponds to encourage the growth of algae, plankton and plants that the fish feed on. This simple and sustainable system has been practised here for around 5,000 years!

NATURE *Threatened Yangtze*

Fish stocks and other wildlife of the Yangtze are today under threat. The increase in fishing is one of the causes, but an increase in river traffic and pollution are also to blame. A clear sign of the problem has been the fall in the commercial fish catch on the Yangtze. In 1954, 434,000 tonnes were caught, but by 2002 this had fallen to less than 100,000 tonnes. In response the government introduced its first ever ban on commercial fishing, between February and May, the months when the fish under threat are breeding.

The most endangered species on the Yangtze is the Baiji river dolphin. This unique dolphin is thought to have lived in

Above: The Baiji river dolphin is so endangered that it might well be extinct by now. Being caught in fishing nets or hit by boats are the main reasons for its decline.

the river for over seventy million years. The number of Baiji in the Yangtze has fallen from over 6,000 in the 1950s to fewer than 100 today. Around half the Baiji have died by getting tangled in fishing nets and drowning (dolphins need to come up for air to breathe). A further third have been killed by collisions with boats and their propellers. In 2000, dolphin experts estimated there may be as few as five Baiji left in the Yangtze. If the experts are right, then it is quite likely that this ancient species of dolphin is by now extinct.

HISTORY *Watering the land*

Quite a lot of the farmland around us is artificially watered, or irrigated, using water from the Yangtze and its lakes and tributaries. Irrigation in China can be traced back for around 4,000 years. Many of the methods used have hardly changed and can still be seen today.

Surface irrigation for example, simply flooding the land from channels dug into the earth, still accounts for ninety-nine per cent of all irrigated farmland in China. Nearly half of this land is used for growing rice, the same crop that irrigation was first developed for all those years ago.

Since 1949 the use of electric or diesel pumps to lift water from rivers and lakes has dramatically increased the amount of irrigated farmland. In fact, by 2000, the area of irrigated land had increased threefold to an amazing fifty-one million hectares – just over half of all China's farmland!

As the demand for food increases, irrigation will continue to expand. By 2050 the area of irrigated farmland is expected to be greater than the size of Japan and the UK combined!

Below: A farmer uses a water-raising device to irrigate his fields. An abandoned waterwheel (in the background) is another traditional method of lifting water.

Above: Transplanting rice from the nursery beds to the paddy fields is back-breaking work. The wide hat protects farmers from the sun.

$ ECONOMY *China's Rice Bowl*

Rice is the staple crop in China and is eaten by almost everyone on a daily basis. There are two main types of rice grown in China – upland rice and wet, or paddy, rice. Upland rice grows like most other grains, but wet rice, as its name suggests grows in level fields, known as paddies, that are flooded with water. Rainfall provides some water, but most comes from irrigation systems like those we have seen along the Yangtze. In China, nearly all paddy rice is dependent on irrigation. Water is drained or pumped from rivers or lakes and distributed to the paddies through a system of channels. When it gets to the paddy, it floods on to the land through an opening or gate in the irrigation channel. In some areas, lifting devices such as water-wheels or scoops are also used to apply the water.

You can see paddy rice growing all around us in this region. In fact, China produces about a third of the world's paddy rice – around 200 million tonnes a year! The plentiful water and warm temperatures make this area so good for rice-farming that it is often known as 'the rice bowl of China'.

PEOPLE *Hard work*!

Growing rice is extremely hard work and has changed little in the past 2,000 years. Farmers sow the rice in a nursery field before transplanting it to a shallow, flooded paddy after four or five weeks. Small earthen walls called 'bunds' are built around the edge of the paddy to contain the water. Farmers increase the depth of the water as the rice grows – normally it reaches a depth of between ten to fifteen centimetres. As the rice grows it needs regular weeding and farmers may apply chemicals to help reduce weeds and pests. After ten to twelve weeks, the rice begins to turn golden, and the farmers break the bunds to drain the paddy.

Above: Few Chinese people go without their daily bowl of rice. Right: Chinese farmers produce a wide variety of vegetables and sell them at the local markets.

The rice is then ready to be harvested, threshed and stored, an event that often involves the whole family. Finally the stalks are dug or ploughed back into the ground using water buffalo, ready for the whole cycle to start again. In this area farmers sometimes grow two rice crops a year. In the cooler winter months, they don't rest! They grow wheat or other crops.

📖 HISTORY *Ancient capital*

As we approach the ancient city of Nanjing, we gaze out onto buildings and industry instead of rice paddies. Nanjing means 'southern capital' and, true to its name, the city has been China's capital at various times in its five or six thousand-year history. In fact the city you see around you has been the capital of ten kingdoms, or dynasties as they are known in China, since AD 229. Nanjing was also the capital of the Republic of China between 1911-1949 until it was replaced by Beijing, the present-day capital.

One of the most striking features of Nanjing is the impressive city walls. They were originally built about 2,500 years ago!

The walls you can see today date back to 1369 when they were strengthened by the first Emperor of the Ming Dynasty. The walls now stretch an amazing thirty-two kilometres around the city, making them the longest city walls in the world!

As you explore the city you will see that it attracts lots of tourists from China and abroad. Most come to see the famous walls, but others come to visit the burial place of Sun Yatsen, the man who founded modern China in 1911.

Below: The mausoleum of Sun Yatsen is a popular attraction in China's ancient capital, Nanjing.

→ CHANGE *Grand Canal*

Around eighty kilometres downstream of Nanjing, we come face to face with China's other great inland waterway, the Grand Canal at the city of Zhenjiang MAP REF: 1 . The canal crosses the Yangtze and runs between Beijing in the north and Hangzhou in the south. At 1,800 kilometres, the Grand Canal is the world's longest man-made waterway. Parts of it date back 2,400 years!

The canal is still a major transport route for grain and other goods. Our grain barge leaves us here and joins others as they travel nose to tail up the canal like a giant mechanical river serpent. Barges cannot currently travel the entire length of the canal due to a build up of sediment. To tackle this problem water engineers will divert water from the Yangtze to raise the level in the canal. Dredging will remove sediment from the worst sections.

In 2000 plans were also announced to extend the canal south of Hangzhou to the port of Ningbo. This is part of the government's hopes to restore the Grand Canal to its former glory.

Left: Boats travel in convoy along the narrow waterways of the Grand Canal – the longest in the world.

We board another passenger ferry for the final part of our journey to the great port city of Shanghai.

6. The Yangtze Delta

WE ARE NOW IN THE VAST Yangtze delta where the river slows and widens in the final stages of its journey. The delta has long been important as a major trading centre, providing the link between the Yangtze and the East China Sea, and beyond that, the Pacific Ocean. Shanghai, one of China's greatest cities, is located at the mouth of the Yangtze, but the whole delta region is densely populated. As China's economy grows, the delta is becoming heavily developed and will play a key role in China's future.

Below: Shanghai's bustling modern streets are a sharp contrast to the rural areas we have travelled through.

NATURE *A watery world*

Deltas are formed as a river slows and deposits its sediment at a rate faster than the sea or ocean is able to carry it away. Over millions of years the Yangtze delta has built up into a vast flat area, crossed by numerous streams and river channels as water struggles to find its way to the sea. The Yangtze widens dramatically in the delta and reaches a width of about eighty kilometres at its mouth.

In the mouth of the Yangtze lies Chongming Island MAP REF: 1 , the largest of several islands found in the Yangtze delta. The island is formed entirely by the deposit of sediment over the years, and it splits the Yangtze into two channels for its final journey to the sea. We stick to the southern channel as we head through the watery world of the delta towards the teeming city of Shanghai.

 PEOPLE *Vertical living*

The Yangtze delta is among China's most densely populated regions, with an average of 568 people per square kilometre. In parts of Shanghai, a city of almost fifteen million, the figure rises to over 50,000 people per square kilometre! The Chinese average is just 136 per square kilometre.

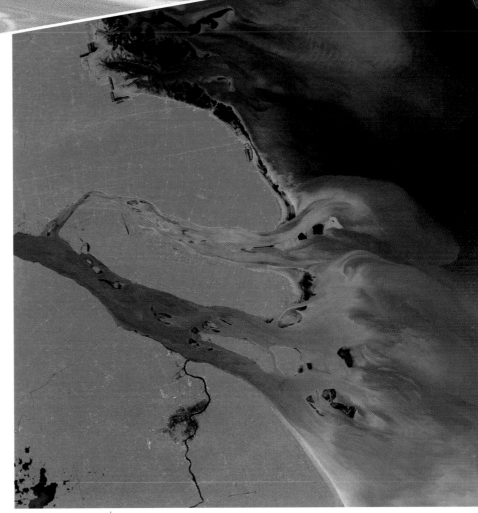

Above: This satellite image clearly shows Chongming Island in the middle of the Yangtze, just before the river reaches the East China Sea.

With so many people, nearly every spare piece of land has been built upon to provide housing, some of which is very crowded. Housing is now spreading onto valuable farmland. But the spread creates new problems. It reduces the amount of food that can be produced.

Planners in the delta region are now turning to the skies for solutions to the delta's growing population. A vertical city has been proposed – a giant skyscraper standing 1,128 metres high and housing 100,000 people on 300 storeys together with shops, offices, cinemas and hospitals.

CHANGE *Into the future*

Our ferry leaves us in Shanghai, China's most important port, which links the Yangtze to the sea. The route into the centre of the city takes us up the Huangpu river as it makes its way to join the Yangtze. We disembark at Shiliupu Wharf and from here take a stroll along the Bund, the main street on the western edge of the Huangpu. The Bund is lined with old buildings from times past when the British, French, Americans and Japanese established trading posts in the city. Across the Huangpu is the special economic zone of Pudong, MAP REF: 2 a shining example of China's new role as a major world economy.

In 1990, Pudong was little more than farmland, but since then it has rapidly developed into a thriving business centre. Covering over one hundred square kilometres, it is an important manufacturing zone for hi-tech industries such as computing and electronics. Pudong is also set to become the financial centre of Asia in the early twenty-first century.

The key to Pudong's success is Waigaoqiao harbour situated on the banks of the Yangtze as it enters the sea. Goods made in Pudong and other regions of China, will be shipped from here throughout the world. Dredging to deepen the channel linking the Yangtze to the sea was completed in 2000 and will make it easier for larger ships to access the ports.

Shanghai and Pudong make it clear that just as the Yangtze was important in China's history, it will be of great importance to its future.

Below: The impressive television tower dominates the landscape of the fast-growing business and industrial district of Pudong. It also marks the end of our journey!

Journey's End

As we wait for our flight home from Pudong's new international airport opened in 1999, we can look out to the point at which the Yangtze meets the East China Sea. What an incredible journey we have had! We have experienced 6,300 kilometres of history and change, seen amazing landscapes and shared in the daily lives of people who live by and depend on the river. It is little wonder that the Chinese are so proud of their great river, the Yangtze.

The Yangtze falls rapidly before levelling off in the second half of its 6,300 kilometre journey.

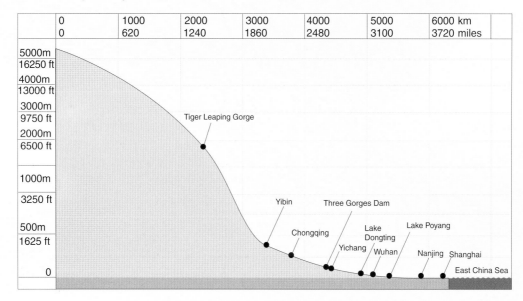

| 0 | 1000 | 2000 | 3000 | 4000 | 5000 | 6000 km |
| 0 | 620 | 1240 | 1860 | 2480 | 3100 | 3720 miles |

Further Information

Useful websites

http://www.pbs.org/itvs/greatwall/
This website discusses the Three Gorges Dam on the Yangtze, provides information on the river and includes an interesting on-line river tour.

http://www.thewaterpage.com/yangtze.htm
This website provides a very good summary of the Yangtze and some of the issues it and its people currently face.

http://en.wikipedia.org/wiki/Naxi
This web page provides additional information about the fascinating Naxi people and their culture and religion.

Books

The Yangtze (Rivers) by Cari Meister (Abdo Publishing Company 2002)

Great Rivers: The Yangtze by Michael Pollard (Evans Brothers 2003)

The Changing Face Of China by Stephen Keeler (Hodder Wayland 2002)

Themes in Geography: Rivers by Fred Martyn (Heinemann Library, 1996)

Earth in Danger: Rivers by Polly Goodman (Hodder Wayland, 2005)

Geography Fact Files: Rivers by Mandy Ross (Hodder Wayland, 2004)

Rivers in Action by Mary Green (Franklin Watts, 2003)

Glossary

Bank The side of a river.

Channel The passage through which a river flows.

Cholera A disease of the gut.

Commercial fish catch Fish caught by the fishing industry that are then sold.

Confluence The place where two rivers meet.

Current The flow of water in a certain direction.

Dam A barrier that holds or diverts water.

Deforestation The clearance of trees from land that was once covered by forest.

Delta A geographical feature at the mouth of a river, formed by the build-up of sediment.

Drainage basin The area of land drained by a river and its tributaries.

Dyke A ridge built alongside a river, sea or lake shore that holds back the water and so reduces flooding.

Erosion The wearing away of land by natural forces such as running water, glaciers, wind or waves.

Faults Lines of natural weakness in the earth's crust.

Flood When a river spills over its banks, onto land that is usually dry.

Funicular railway A railway whose carriages are pulled along by a cable and pulley system.

Glacier A mass of snow and ice.

Gorge A deep, narrow river valley with steep, rocky sides.

Headwaters Water at the source of a river.

Hydroelectric Power (H.E.P.) Electricity generated by water as it passes through turbines. HEP involves damming river valleys and forming artificial lakes.

Irrigation The artificial application of water to crops to make up for low or unpredictable rainfall.

Lock An enclosed section of river, where the water level can be raised or lowered. This process helps ships move up or down the river.

Meander A large bend in a river.

Meltwater Water produced by the melting of snow and ice.

Municipality Town, city or district that has its own local government.

Ox-bow lake A small arc-shaped lake that was once part of the former course of a river.

Paddy fields Fields that are usually covered with shallow water, where rice is grown.

Peninsula A narrow piece of land that sticks out from the mainland into a river, lake or sea. A peninsula is surrounded by water on at least three sides.

Population density The number of people living in a given area.

Rapids Fast-moving stretches of water.

Reservoir An artificial lake that forms when water collects behind a dam. Reservoir water may be used for irrigation or for producing hydro-electric power.

Run-off Rainwater that runs off the earth's surface into rivers, streams and lakes.

Sedan chair An enclosed chair fixed to two poles that is carried by porters. Historically this luxury was reserved for Emperors and high noblemen.

Sediment Fine sand and earth that is moved and left by water, wind or ice.

Sewage Waste carried by sewers for treatment or disposal. Sewage normally includes human waste and waste water, but it can include chemicals from homes, offices and factories.

Shoal An underwater sandbank.

Sluice gates Gates that control the flow of water and sediment in a river channel when opened or closed.

Staple crops Foods that form the basis of people's diets.

Subsistence farming Farming that provides food mainly for the farmer's household. Surplus food may be sold.

Terraced farming A system of growing crops on horizontal steps cut into a hillside.

Tributary A stream or river that flows into another larger stream or river.

Waterfall A sudden fall of water over a steep drop.

Waterway A body of water such as a river or canal that is used as a transport route.

Index